Bible Promises for Kids

*Presented to*_____

*Given by*_____

_____

_____

*Date*_____

Your word is a lamp for my
feet and a light on my path.
Psalm 119:105

Bible
Promises
for Kids

PUBLISHING GROUP

Nashville, Tennessee

Bible Promises for Kids

Broadman & Holman Publishers, Nashville, Tennessee
ISBN 978-0-8054-2740-0

Dewey Decimal Classification: 242.5
Subject Heading: God–Promises/Promises/Children

Printed in the United States
8 9 10 11 10 09 08 07

Contents

Promises for Every Day
When You're Waking 8
Why You're Learning 14
How You're Choosing 20
What You're Thinking 26
Where You're Going 32

Promises for Afternoons and Weekends
When You're Indoors 40
When You're Outdoors 46
When You're Bored 52
When You're Scared 58
When You're Tired 64

Promises Bigger than You Are
Obeying Your Parents 72
Loving Your Family 78
Seeing Your Friends 84
Sharing Your Life 90

Promises that Last Forever
Being in Church 98
Wanting to Worship 104
Bowing in Prayer 110
Reading the Bible 116
Believing in God 122

Promises
for
Every Day

If for any reason, you've picked up the idea along the way that the Bible doesn't really apply to your life, that it's mostly just a bunch of stories plopped in the middle of a bunch of other words you can't understand, then you've come to the right place.

This little book is pretty much *all* Bible verses. But if you promise to keep reading, you'll see for yourself that God's Word has your name written all over it.

When You're Waking

You're Sure it's Time to Get Up Already?

Satisfy us in the morning
  with Your faithful love
    so that we may shout with joy
      and be glad all our days.

Psalm 90:14

What's the first thing you
think about in the morning?
*Verses like these can help you remember
to make "Thank You, God" the first words
to come out of your mouth every day.*

The LORD's faithful love does not
cease; His compassions have no end.
They are new every morning; great is
Your faithfulness.

Lamentations 3:22-23

It is good to praise the LORD, to
sing praise to Your name, Most High,
to declare Your faithful love in the
morning and Your faithfulness at night.

Psalm 92:1-2

The minute you wake up,
God is there. He's always there.
And because of that, your day can start
looking up before you even get to the
breakfast table.

When they became fully awake, they
saw His glory.

Luke 9:32

When I awake, I will be satisfied with
Your presence.

Psalm 17:15

When I wake up, I am still with You.

Psalm 139:18

But some days start out a little darker and cloudier than others. *That's when you need to go ahead and ask God right off the bat to help you with whatever it is that's worrying you.*

At daybreak, LORD, You hear my voice; at daybreak I plead my case to You and watch expectantly.

Psalm 5:3

Be our strength every morning, and our salvation in time of trouble.

Isaiah 33:2

The LORD will protect your coming and going both now and forever.

Psalm 121:8

Wake up, my soul!
  Wake up, harp and lyre!
I will wake up the dawn. I will praise
  You, LORD, among the peoples;
I will sing praises to You
  among the nations.
For Your faithful love is as high
  as the heavens; Your faithfulness
  reaches to the clouds.
God, be exalted above the heavens;
  let Your glory be over the whole earth.

Psalm 57:7-11

So hop on up and be glad that
God has your day in total control.
*And nothing that can happen between
now and nighttime will keep Him from
loving and caring for you.*

The day is Yours, also the night;
You established the moon and the sun.

Psalm 74:16

I lie down and sleep; I wake again
because the LORD sustains me.

Psalm 3:5

At this I awoke and looked around.
My sleep had been most pleasant to me.

Jeremiah 31:26

Why You're Learning

What's So Important about School Stuff?

A house is built by wisdom,
   and it is established by understanding;
   by knowledge the rooms are filled
      with every precious and
      beautiful treasure.

Proverbs 24:3-4

Every day is a chance to learn something new about God.
The wonders of science, the order of math, even the names and dates of history can show you God in action.

Stop and ponder God's wonders. Do you know how God controls them or makes his storm cloud flash with lightning?

Job 37:14-15

The heavens declare the glory of God, and the sky proclaims the work of His hands. Day after day they pour out speech; night after night they communicate knowledge.

Psalm 19:1-2

**Everything that's true
really comes from the Lord.**
*That means God is involved in every class
you take, helping you see His truth all
over the place.*

If any of you lacks wisdom, he should
ask God, who gives to all generously.

James 1:5

The fear of the LORD is the
beginning of wisdom; all who follow
His instructions have good insight.

Psalm 111:10

When you learn something, it just makes you feel good.
God has designed you to grow and stretch, to enjoy the experience of knowing more than you did yesterday.

Instruct a wise man, and he will be wiser still; teach a righteous man, and he will learn more.

Proverbs 9:9

For the one who finds [wisdom] finds life and obtains favor from the LORD.

Proverbs 8:32-35

Doesn't He look with favor on all the wise of heart?

Job 37:24

My son, if you accept
   my words and store up
   my commands within you,
   listening closely to wisdom
   and directing your heart
   to understanding;
furthermore, if you call out to insight
   and lift your voice to understanding,
   if you seek it like silver and
   search for it like hidden treasure,
   then you will understand the fear
   of the LORD and discover the
   knowledge of God.

Proverbs 2:1-5

Even when it's dull and boring, learning is a matter of obedience.
You're going to be doing school a big part of today anyway. Why not use the time to please God with your mind?

Hold on to instruction; don't let go. Guard it, for it is your life.

Proverbs 4:13

Grow in the grace and knowledge of our Lord and Savior Jesus Christ.

2 Peter 3:18

So that you may walk worthy of the Lord, fully pleasing to Him, bearing fruit in every good work and growing in the knowledge of God.

Colossians 1:10

How You're Choosing

What's the Trick to Making Decisions?

May the words of my mouth
and the meditation of my heart
be acceptable to You, O LORD,
my rock and my Redeemer.

Psalm 19:14

**The Bible is always
the best place to start.**
*You don't have to understand it all to
learn—little by little—that everything in
God's Word is true and for your best.*

You must follow the LORD your God
and fear Him. You must keep His commands and listen to His voice; you must
serve Him and remain faithful to Him.
Deuteronomy 13:4

Then you will understand righteousness,
justice, and integrity—every good path.
For wisdom will enter your heart, and
knowledge will delight your soul.
Proverbs 2:9-10

Whenever you're in doubt, don't be afraid to ask someone you trust. *Go to your parents, teachers, people who have lived enough to know what they're talking about.*

A fool's way is right in his own eyes, but whoever listens to counsel is wise.

Proverbs 12:15

A wise warrior is better than a strong one, and a man of knowledge than one of strength; for you should wage war with sound guidance—victory comes with many counselors.

Proverbs 24:5-6

Never be fooled into thinking that bad choices will work out better. *What some people call fun is what God often calls sin. And He wants to protect you from the pain it always causes.*

Don't be jealous of sinners; instead, always fear the LORD. For then you will have a future, and your hope will never fade.

Proverbs 23:17-18

God is faithful and He will not allow you to be tempted beyond what you are able, but with the temptation He will also provide a way of escape, so that you are able to bear it.

1 Corinthians 10:13

How can a young man keep
his way pure? By keeping Your word.
I have sought You with all my heart;
don't let me wander from
Your commands.
I have treasured Your word in my heart
so that I may not sin against You. . . .
I will meditate on Your precepts
and think about Your ways.
I will delight in Your statutes;
I will not forget Your word.

Psalm 119:9-11, 15-16

Nothing makes God happier than seeing you put your trust in Him.
He offers you a level path, a straight way, a sure shot to the places He wants you to go. So why go anywhere else?

Even a young man is known by his actions—by whether his behavior is pure and upright.

Proverbs 20:11

Show me Your way, LORD, and lead me on a level path.

Psalm 27:11

You welcome the one who joyfully does what is right.

Isaiah 64:5

What You're Thinking

Some Things Are So Hard to Understand

I pray this: that your love
   will keep on growing in knowledge . . .
   so that you can determine
   what really matters.

Philippians 1:9-10

The Bible can help you understand your biggest questions in life.
You can learn so much by reading the Bible every day and by listening carefully to those who teach it to you.

We know that the Son of God has come and has given us understanding so that we may know the true One.

1 John 5:20

His disciples did not understand these things at first.

John 12:16

Then He opened their minds to understand the Scriptures.

Luke 24:45

God is so much bigger than our minds can reach around.

You're not the only one who struggles to understand. God's ways are just higher than ours.

There are some matters that are hard to understand.

2 Peter 3:16

"For My thoughts are not your thoughts, and your ways are not My ways," declares the LORD. "For as heaven is higher than earth, so My ways are higher than your ways."

Isaiah 55:8-9

There are some things in life you simply have to accept by faith.
And if you are a believer in Christ, you can be sure your faith is in Someone who will always take care of you.

Jesus answered, "What I'm doing you don't understand now, but afterward you will know."

John 13:7

By faith we understand.

Hebrews 11:3

What no eye has seen and no ear has heard, and what has never come into a man's heart, is what God has prepared for those who love Him.

1 Corinthians 2:9

This is what the LORD says,
  "The wise must not boast
    in his wisdom; the mighty
    must not boast in his might;
    the rich must not boast in his riches.
  "But the one who
    boasts should boast in this,
    that he understands and knows
    Me, that I am the LORD, who
    acts in faithful love, justice, and
    righteousness on the earth.
  "For in these things I delight,"
    says the LORD.

Jeremiah 9:23-24

God will show you what you need to know when you're ready for it.
So don't worry. Do your best, but then rest in the wonderful fact that God knows you, and God knows everything.

Don't worry about anything, but in everything, through prayer and petition with thanksgiving, let your requests be made known to God. And the peace of God, which surpasses every thought, will guard your hearts and your minds in Christ Jesus.

Philippians 4:6-7

For He scans the ends of the earth; He sees everything under all the heavens.

Job 28:24

Where You're Going

Wonder Who I'll Be When I Grow Up?

"For I know the plans
    I have for you," says the LORD,
        "wholesome plans and not harmful,
            to give you a future and hope."

Jeremiah 29:11

One thing's for sure: You can trust God to show you the way. *The best kind of attitude to have about your future is peace, because God has promised to let you know His will.*

Reveal to me the way I should go.
Psalm 143:8

Then we will no longer be little children, tossed by the waves and blown around by every wind of teaching.
Ephesians 4:14

You will keep in perfect peace the mind that is dependent on You, for it is trusting in You.

Isaiah 26:3

Growing up isn't easy, but it's God's plan for making you stronger. *You can come up against some pretty tough challenges, but God can make them work for you.*

Commit your activities to the LORD and your plans will be achieved.

Proverbs 16:3

The testing of your faith produces endurance. But endurance must do its complete work, so that you may be mature and complete, lacking nothing.

James 1:3-4

Where You're Going

Keep your eye on people who are growing up and staying faithful. *Learn from those who are trusting God with their lives. They'll help you see that you can trust God with yours.*

Watch the blameless and observe the upright.

Psalm 37:37

The path of the righteous is like the light of dawn, shining brighter and brighter until midday.

Proverbs 4:18

Take delight in the LORD, and He will give you your heart's desires.

Psalm 37:4

I will praise You because I am
　　unique in remarkable ways.
Your works are wonderful,
　　and I know this very well.
My bones were not hidden from You
　　when I was made in secret,
　　when I was formed in
　　the depths of the earth.
Your eyes saw me when I was formless;
　　all my days were written in Your
　　book and planned before a
　　single one of them began.

Psalm 139:14-16

Where You're Going

God loves you so much, and He has a great future planned for you. *You may have an idea for what you want to do in life. But God knows already. And it will be something special.*

A man's heart plans his way, but the LORD determines his steps.

Proverbs 16:9

LORD my God, You have done many things—Your wonderful works and Your plans for us; none can compare with You. If I were to report and speak of them, they are more than can be told.

Psalm 40:5

Promises
for Afternoons
and Weekends

Not every day is a school day *(whew!)*, and not every hour is a working hour. So how do you decide what to do with your down time? Does your faith in God come into play when you're just playing?

The same way God is there to help you through the hours of a school day, He is also there to help you through every other hour of every other day—not to snoop and snap His fingers at you, but to keep you safe, to keep you at peace.

When You're Indoors

What's Up When School's Out?

Whether you eat or drink,
  or whatever you do,
    do everything for God's glory.

1 Corinthians 10:31

Be careful what you're watching— what you're letting into your mind. *Television and video games can make for a lot of fun, but be careful: they can also make for bad company.*

I will live with integrity of heart in my house. I will not set anything godless before my eyes.

Psalm 101:2-3

Be careful that you are not enticed to turn aside.

Deuteronomy 11:16

Don't share in the sins of others. Keep yourself pure.

1 Timothy 5:22

There's not a whole lot to be gained from goofing off.
Having fun is a big part of being a kid. But don't let your brain and body just turn to mush.

Because of utter laziness, the roof caves in, because of idle hands, the house leaks.
Eccleasiates 10:18

The slacker buries his hand in the bowl; he is too weary to bring it to his mouth.
Proverbs 26:14-15

A lazy person will go hungry.
Proverbs 19:15

Part of being in a family means taking your share of responsibility. *There's a lot you can do around the house to help make your mom and dad's life a whole lot more pleasant.*

For we hear that there are some among you who walk irresponsibly, not working at all, but interfering with the work of others. Now we command and exhort such people, by the Lord Jesus Christ, that quietly working, they may eat their own bread.

2 Thessalonians 3:11-12

The son who gathers during summer is prudent; the son who sleeps during harvest is disgraceful.

Proverbs 10:5

Make every effort to supplement
your faith with goodness,
goodness with knowledge,
knowledge with self-control,
self-control with endurance,
endurance with godliness,
godliness with brotherly affection,
and brotherly affection with love.
For if these qualities are yours and are
increasing, they will keep you from
being useless or unfruitful in the
knowledge of our Lord Jesus Christ.

2 Peter 1:5-8

More than anything, make sure your down time is still God's time. *The happiest kids are not the ones who do whatever they want, but the ones who do whatever their Father asks.*

Finally brothers, whatever is true, whatever is honorable, whatever is just, whatever is pure, whatever is lovely, whatever is commendable—if there is any moral excellence and if there is any praise—dwell on these things.

Philippians 4:8

Then my people will dwell in a peaceful place, and in safe and restful dwellings.

Isaiah 32:18

When You're Outdoors

God? You Really Created All This?

The streets of the city will be filled
with boys and girls playing in them. . . .
They will be My people, and I will be
their God in truth and righteousness.
Zechariah 8:5, 8

Always remember who gives you the strength to run and jump and play. *God loves you enough to fill you with the energy to enjoy His creation. So get out there in it—and take Him with you!*

All things were created through Him, and apart from Him not one thing was created that has been created.

John 1:3

In His hand is the life of every living thing and the spirit of all human flesh.

Job 12:10

For in Him we live and move and exist.

Acts 17:28

**Everything you see around you
is a gift from your heavenly Father.**
*God made it all—every leaf and branch,
every rock, snowflake, and creekbed. He's
something else!*

In the beginning God created the
heavens and the earth.

Genesis 1:1

He formed the earth and made it; He
established it; He did not create it to be
empty, but formed it to be inhabited.

Isaiah 45:18

Why would God go to so much trouble to be so incredibly creative? *All the shapes and colors, sounds and textures—even the sticky stuff on a bug's legs—are there to make us think of Him.*

I will put cypress trees in the desert, elms and box trees together, so that all may see and know, consider and understand, that the hand of the LORD has done this.

Isaiah 41:19-20

For He Is here—the One who forms the mountains, creates the wind, and reveals His thoughts to man; the One who makes the dawn out of darkness and strides on the heights of the earth.

Amos 4:13

When I observe Your heavens,
  the work of Your fingers,
  the moon and the stars,
  which You set in place,
  what is man, that You remember him,
  the son of man, that You look after him?
You made him little less than God and
  crowned him with glory and honor. . . .
O LORD, our Lord, how magnificent
  is Your name throughout the earth!

Psalm 8:3-5, 9

So whenever you're outside, take a look around. You've got company. *Thank God for making the sky so blue, the air so clear, the day just right for having fun in His beautiful world.*

Remember your Creator in the days of your youth.

Ecclesiastes 12:1

God, You are worthy to receive glory and honor and power, because You have created all things, and because of Your will they exist and were created.

Revelation 4:11

From the rising of the sun to its setting, let the name of the LORD be praised.

Psalm 113:3

When You're Bored

I've Looked! There's Nothing to Do!

The imperishable quality
   of a gentle and quiet spirit . . .
      is very valuable in God's eyes.

1 Peter 3:4

Today's the only today you have.
Make something special out of it.
If you're feeling particularly bored, one of the best ways to work yourself out of it is to do what's there—and do it well.

Pay careful attention, then, to how you walk—not as unwise people but as wise—making the most of the time.

Ephesians 5:15-16

Listen, my son, and be wise; keep your mind on the right course.

Proverbs 23:19

All that your hands find to accomplish, accomplish it with your own strength.

Ecclesiastes 9:10

**Ever get a little bored in church?
Try your best to listen anyway.**
*It may not always be very exciting, but the
things you hear today will soon make a lot
more sense.*

Listen closely, pay attention to the
words of the wise, and apply your mind
to my knowledge.

Proverbs 22:17

You will do well to pay attention to it,
as to a lamp shining in a dismal place,
until the day dawns and the morning
star arises in your hearts.

2 Peter 1:19

I know it may sound crazy, but being quiet can be a good thing.
You'd be surprised what you and God can do together when no one else is around, when it's just you and Him.

Don't let your spirit be easily grieved....
Don't ask, "Why were the old days better than these?"

Ecclesiastes 7:9, 10

Better a dry crust with peace than a house full of feasting with strife.

Proverbs 17:1

Seek to lead a quiet life, to mind your own business, and to work with your own hands.

1 Thessalonians 4:11

You will be delivered by returning
and resting; your strength will lie
in quiet confidence.
But you are not willing.
You say, "No!
We will escape on horses. . . .
We will ride on fast horses"—but
those who pursue you will be fast. . . .
Therefore the LORD is waiting to show
you mercy, and is rising up to show
you compassion, for the
LORD is a just God.
Happy are all who
wait patiently for Him.

Isaiah 30:15-16, 18

So be patient, and wait for the great things God has in store for you.
Life can't be a hop, skip, and a jump all the time. Sometimes God just knows you need a little peace and quiet.

Come now, you who say, "Today or tomorrow we will travel to such and such a city and spend a year there and do business and make a profit.". . . Instead, you should say, "If the Lord wills, we will live and do this or that."
James 4:13, 15

See how the farmer waits for the precious fruit of the earth and is patient with it until it receives the early and the late rains. You also must be patient.
James 5:7-8

When You're Scared

Is There Any Way to Not Feel Afraid?

When I am afraid,
  I will trust in You.
    In God, whose word I praise,
      in God I trust; I will not fear.

Psalm 56:3-4

Fear can be a big problem, but it's not as big as God's love for you. *He is so powerful, and you mean so much to Him—more than you can ever know. Count on Him to help you.*

Do not be afraid or dismayed, for the Lord your God is with you wherever you go.

Joshua 1:9

Aren't two sparrows sold for a penny? Yet not one of them falls to the ground without your Father's consent. But even the hairs of your head have all been counted. Don't be afraid therefore; you are worth more than many sparrows.

Matthew 10:29-31

Nighttime can be frightening, but God is there. He's not sleeping. *He is like a blanket, a cool sip of water, whatever you need to make you feel safe and secure.*

My God illuminates my darkness.

Psalm 18:28

Even the darkness is not too dark for You. The night shines like the day; darkness and light are alike to You.

Psalm 139:12

The LORD will be your confidence.

Proverbs 3:26

Sometimes other people can make you afraid—afraid to be yourself.
Big prophets like Jeremiah and Ezekiel, who wrote these verses, could even feel that way. But God promised to be there.

Do not say, "I am only a youth," for you will go wherever I send you and speak whatever I tell you. Do not be afraid of anyone, for I will be with you to deliver you.

Jeremiah 1:7-8

Do not be afraid of their words, and do not be dismayed by their looks. . . . But speak My words to them, whether they listen or refuse to listen.

Ezekiel 2:6-7

God is our refuge and strength,
   a helper who is always found
   in times of trouble.
Therefore we will not be afraid,
   though the earth trembles
   and the mountains topple
   into the depths of the seas,
   though its waters roar and foam
   and the mountains quake
   with its turmoil. . . .
"Know that I am God, exalted among
   the nations, exalted on the earth."
The LORD of Hosts is with us;
   the God of Jacob is our stronghold.

Psalm 46:1-3, 10-11

When You're Scared

Fear is just a big lie. The truth is, God will always take care of you. *He's your hope, He's your helper. He's your Father, He's your friend. And He is here right now, right where you are.*

The LORD is my light and my salvation—whom should I fear? The LORD is the stronghold of my life—of whom should I be afraid?

Psalm 27:1

When I walk through the darkest valley, I fear no danger, for You are with me.

Psalm 23:4

For God has not given us a spirit of fearfulness.

2 Timothy 1:7

When You're Tired

Boy, This Has Sure Been a Long Day

I pray that He may grant you,
   according to the riches of His glory,
      to be strengthened with power
         through His Spirit.

Ephesians 3:16

Out of breath? Low on energy?
Ask God for something extra.
Tired arms and legs are part of growing
up, but trusting God to give you strength
makes you strong to the bone.

Strengthen the weak hands, steady the
shaking knees! Say to the faint-hearted:
"Be strong; do not fear!"

Isaiah 35:3-4

God—He clothes me with strength. . . .
You widen a place beneath me for my
steps, and my ankles do not give way.

Psalm 18:32, 36

With You I can attack a barrier,
and with my God I can leap a wall.

Psalm 18:29

Some people's words make you want to quit. But not God's Word. *The Bible tells us about people who had good reasons to give up . . . and one good Reason not to.*

For all of them were trying to intimidate us, saying, "They will become discouraged in the work, and it will never be finished." But now, my God, strengthen my hands.

Nehemiah 6:9

Strengthen me through Your word.

Psalm 119:28

When You're Tired

Jesus is your best example. He knew how to keep His eyes on the Father. *This is a long passage, but it's such a good one. It's God reminding you to look up when your strength is running down.*

Since we also have such a large cloud of witnesses surrounding us, let us lay aside every weight and the sin that so easily ensnares us, and run with endurance the race that lies before us, keeping our eyes on Jesus, the source and perfecter of our faith, who for the joy that lay before Him endured a cross and despised the shame, and has sat down at the right hand of God's throne. For consider Him who endured such hostility from sinners against Himself, so that you won't grow weary and lose heart.

Hebrews 12:1-3

Have you not heard?
He is the everlasting God, the Creator
   of the earth from end to end.
He never grows faint or weary;
   there is no limit to His understanding.
He gives strength to the weary,
   and strengthens the powerless.
Youths may faint and grow weary,
   and young men stumble and fall,
   but those who trust in the LORD
   will renew their strength;
they will soar on wings like eagles;
   they will run and not grow weary;
   they will walk and not faint.

Isaiah 40:28-31

Weakness is God's way of letting us lean a little harder on Him.
So the next time you're feeling wrung out, let that feeling be your reminder that you need God's strength for everything.

Do not fear, for I am with you;
do not be afraid, for I am your God.
I will strengthen you; I will help you;
I will support you with My righteous
right hand.

Isaiah 41:10

Therefore, I will most gladly boast all
the more about my weaknesses, so that
Christ's power may reside in me. . . .
For when I am weak, then I am strong.

2 Corinthians 12:9, 10

Promises Bigger than You Are

God, in His love and care for you, has placed you in a family. Still, it's not always easy to get along with everybody, is it?

He's also given you friends, people who are on the same page with your favorite interests and activities. Still, even a good friend can be difficult sometimes.

Living and dealing with others requires unselfishness and patience. And rewards you with some of life's greatest blessings.

Obeying Your Parents

I Have a Feeling This Is for My Good

Children, obey your parents in the Lord, because this is right. "Honor your father and mother"—which is the first commandment with a promise—"that it may go well with you."

Ephesians 6:1-3

Being obedient to your parents
is part of being obedient to God.
*It makes the Lord happy to see you doing
what your parents tell you. It makes your
parents happier people, too.*

Children, obey your parents in everything, for this is pleasing in the Lord.
Colossians 3:20

As obedient children, do not be
conformed to the desires of your former
ignorance but, as the One who called
you is holy, you also are to be holy
in all your conduct.
1 Peter 1:14-15

Remember therefore what you have
received and heard.
Revelation 3:3

Do you know what your parent's discipline tells you about them?
By caring enough to correct you, they are proving they love you even more than their own popularity.

No discipline seems enjoyable at the time, but painful. Later on, however, it yields the fruit of peace and righteousness to those who have been trained by it.

Hebrews 12:11

When you walk, your steps will not be hindered; when you run, you will not stumble.

Proverbs 4:12

Doing things your way may seem better, but the fun won't last long. *Disobeying always just gets you into more trouble—and makes your parents have to be that much more stern with you.*

Do not be like a horse or mule, without understanding, that must be controlled with bit and bridle, or else it will not come near you.

Psalm 32:9

Obey your leaders and submit to them, for they keep watch over your souls as those who will give an account, so that they can do this with joy and not with grief, for that would be unprofitable for you.

Hebrews 13:17

Promises Bigger than You Are

Keep your father's command, and
    don't reject your mother's teaching.
Always bind them to your heart;
    tie them around your neck.
When you walk here and there,
    they will guide you;
when you lie down,
    they will watch over you;
when you wake up,
    they will talk to you.
For a commandment is a lamp,
    teaching is a light,
    and corrective instructions
    are the way to life.

Proverbs 6:20-23

Just look at all the things that come your way when you're doing right. *These verses give you a few good hints, and you'll think of even more when you start seeing what obedience can do.*

Don't forget my teaching, but let your heart keep my commands; for they will bring you many days, a full life, and well-being.

Proverbs 3:1-2

Keep the LORD's commands and statutes I am giving you today, for your own good.

Deuteronomy 10:13

Keep my commands and live.

Proverbs 4:4

Promises Bigger than You Are

Loving Your Family

I Assume This Means Brothers and Sisters

Let us no longer criticize one another,
but instead decide not to put a stumbling
block or pitfall in your brother's way.

Romans 14:13

**Families are a gift from God—
His way to surround us with love.**
*He knew we would be lonely without each
other, so He put us together in families—
so we could love one another.*

God provides homes for those who are
deserted.

Psalm 68:6

He gives the childless woman a household, making her the joyful mother of
children.

Psalm 113:9

How good and pleasant it is when
brothers can live together!

Psalm 133:1

Your family has needs that God intends to be met through you.

Why should we care what happens to our brother or sister? Because it's the Bible's clear command.

If a brother or sister is without clothes and lacks daily food, and one of you says to them, "Go in peace, keep warm, and eat well," but you don't give them what the body needs, what good is it?

James 2:15-16

You yourselves are taught by God to love one another.

1 Thessalonians 4:9

Your family really deserves your first attention—even before your friends. *The Bible says that one of the best places to practice our Christian faith is with the people under our own roof.*

If anyone does not provide for his own relatives, and especially for his household, he has denied the faith.

1 Timothy 5:8

They should learn to practice their religion toward their own family first and to repay their parents, for this pleases God.

1 Timothy 5:4

No city or house divided against itself will stand.

Matthew 12:25

Do not judge, so that you won't be judged. For with the judgment you use, you will be judged, and with the measure you use, it will be measured to you.

Why do you look at the speck in your brother's eye, but don't notice the log in your own eye?

Or how can you say to your brother, "Let me take the speck out of your eye," and look, there's a log in your eye?

Hypocrite! First take the log out of your eye, and then you will see clearly to take the speck out of your brother's eye.

Matthew 7:1-5

Home should be a place of peace, where everyone is safe and secure. *It's a place to talk about God and how much He loves us—and to work to make sure He's at home at our house.*

We must work for the good of all, especially for those who belong to the household of faith.

Galatians 6:10

Go back home to your own people, and report to them how much the Lord has done for you and how He has had mercy on you.

Mark 5:19

May there be peace within your walls.

Psalm 122:7

Seeing Your Friends

What Are the Rules of Good Friendship?

Two are better than one . . . for if one of them falls, his companion can help him up. But woe to the one who falls alone with no one to help him up.

Ecclesiastes 4:9-10

The best kind of friends are
the ones who build each other up.
*Try thinking less about what your friends
do for you and your fun, and more about
what you can do for them and their good.*

Each one of us must please his neighbor for his good, in order to build him
up. For even the Messiah did not please
Himself.

Romans 15:2-3

So then, we must pursue what promotes
peace.

Romans 14:19

Everything, dear friends, is for building
you up.

2 Corinthians 12:19

If there's anything a friend is for,
it's to help each other in tough times.
*Not every day is a game in the back yard.
When a friend needs help, be sure you're
there to give it.*

A friend loves at all times.

Proverbs 17:17

Don't abandon your friend. . . . Better a
neighbor nearby than a brother far away.

Proverbs 27:10

A despairing man should receive loyalty
from his friends.

Job 6:14

Not everyone makes a good friend or helps you to be a good person.
You can be nice to everybody, but be sure the friends you spend the most time with are people you should want to be like.

Do not be deceived: "Bad company corrupts good morals."
1 Corinthians 15:33

I implore you, brothers, watch out for those. . . . Avoid them; for such people do not serve our Lord Christ but their own appetites.
Romans 16:17-18

I am a friend to all who fear You, to those who keep Your precepts.
Psalm 119:63

Therefore, God's chosen ones, holy and loved, put on heartfelt compassion, kindness, humility, gentleness, and patience, accepting one another and forgiving one another if anyone has a complaint against another.

Just as the Lord has forgiven you, so also you must forgive.

Above all, put on love—the perfect bond of unity. And let the peace of the Messiah, to which you were also called in one body, control your hearts.

Colossians 3:12-15

Being a friend can take hard work, but the reward is really worth it.
We can learn from Jesus and others in the Bible that friends are people who go out of their way. It should always be like that.

Jesus loved Martha, her sister, and Lazarus. So when He heard that he was sick, He stayed two more days in the place where He was.

John 11:5

The LORD restored Job's losses when he interceded for his friends.

Job 42:10

If there is any other commandment— all are summed up by this: "You shall love your neighbor as yourself."

Romans 13:9

Sharing Your Life

What Should Others Expect from Me?

Little children,
we must not love
in word or speech,
but in deed and truth.

1 John 3:18

The sooner you become a giver,
the more smiles you'll get to enjoy.
Our stuff only tends to pile up or get lost.
A better plan for the things we have is to
use them to meet needs in others' lives.

Don't neglect to do good and to share,
for God is pleased with such sacrifices.

Hebrews 13:16

Give to the one who asks you, and don't
turn away from the one who wants to
borrow from you.

Matthew 5:42

Be merciful, just as your Father also is
merciful.

Luke 6:36

You may not have much money, but there's plenty of "you" to go around. *Just share what you have—your time, your concern, your attention, your afternoon, anything!*

We cared so much for you that we were pleased to share with you not only the gospel of God but also our own lives, because you had become dear to us.

1 Thessalonians 2:8

I will most gladly spend and be spent for you.

2 Corinthians 12:15

**Make time for the other kids
that nobody else does anything for.**
*Hanging around unpopular people may
make you look dumb in some folks' eyes,
but it makes you look great in God's.*

One who isolates himself pursues
selfish desires.

Proverbs 18:1

For if you love those who love you,
what reward will you have? . . . And if
you greet only your brothers, what are
you doing out of the ordinary?

Matthew 5:46-47

Just as you want others to do for you,
do the same for them.

Luke 6:31

Remember this: the person who sows sparingly will also reap sparingly, and the person who sows generously will also reap generously.

Each person should do as he has decided in his heart—not out of regret or out of necessity, for God loves a cheerful giver.

And God is able to make every grace overflow to you, so that in every way, always having everything you need, you may excel in every good work.

2 Corinthians 9:6-8

The love and concern you invest in other people will come back to you. *The Bible says that we reap what we sow, that when we put others first, we don't come in last—we get the best blessing!*

Do not grow weary in doing good.

2 Thessalonians 3:13

No rotten talk should come from your mouth, but only what is good for the building up of someone in need, in order to give grace to those who hear.

Ephesians 4:29

May the Lord cause you to increase and overflow with love for one another and for everyone.

1 Thessalonians 3:12

Promises That Last Forever

It's kind of neat to think that you can be doing things today that you'll be doing the rest of your life—things like going to church, reading your Bible, praying to your heavenly Father.

You know what's even neater than that, though? The fact that your relationship with God lasts way beyond the rest of your life—and all the way to forever.

These last pages will help you think about that for a while. See you later?

Being in Church

What Makes Sundays So Important?

Better a day in Your courts
  than a thousand anywhere else.
I would rather be at the door of the
  house of my God than to live
  in the tents of the wicked.

Psalm 84:10

They call it God's house because
it's where He lives with His family.
*Your church is more than a building on a
street corner. It's a special place for you to
worship God and get to know Him better.*

How happy are those who reside in
Your house, who praise You continually.
Psalm 84:4

Planted in the house of the LORD,
they thrive in the courtyards of our
God. They will still bear fruit in
old age, healthy and green.
Psalm 92:13-14

LORD, I love the house where You dwell,
the place where Your glory resides.
Psalm 26:8

Church is a place where everyone's welcome, where no one's left out.
Don't just go to church wondering what you're going to do there. Go to help others feel cared for.

You are all one in Christ Jesus.
Galatians 3:28

Therefore encourage one another and build each other up.
1 Thessalonians 5:11

Rejoice with those who rejoice; weep with those who weep.
Romans 12:15

**You're never too young to be
a big part of your church family.**
*You don't have to be a grown-up before
you matter at church. You'd be surprised
what good you can do—even at your age!*

No one should despise your youth;
instead, you should be an example to
the believers in speech, in conduct, in
love, in faith, in purity.

1 Timothy 4:12

We who are many are one body in
Christ and individually members of
one another.

Romans 12:5

Seek to excel in building up the church.

1 Corinthians 14:12

Through Him we both have access by one Spirit to the Father. So then you are no longer foreigners and strangers, but fellow citizens with the saints, and members of God's household, built on the foundation of the apostles and prophets, with Christ Jesus Himself as the cornerstone.

The whole building is being fitted together in Him and is growing into a holy sanctuary in the Lord, in whom you also are being built together for God's dwelling in the Spirit.

Ephesians 2:18-22

**Some people can take it or leave it.
But be one who can't do without it.**
*It'll mean more to you as you grow older,
but start looking for reasons to love the
Lord's house now. It's a great place to live!*

Let us be concerned about one
another in order to promote love and
good works, not staying away from our
meetings, as some habitually do, but
encouraging each other, and all the
more as you see the day drawing near.
Hebrews 10:24-25

I rejoiced with those who said to me,
"Let us go to the house of the LORD."
Psalm 122:1

Wanting to Worship

I Really Do Want to Say Thanks

My mouth will tell
about Your righteousness
and Your salvation all day long,
though I cannot sum them up.

Psalm 71:15

How many reasons could you think of to praise your heavenly Father? *For keeping you well, putting food on the table, choosing nice greens and blues to blanket His world. You think of some!*

The LORD is my shepherd;
there is nothing I lack.

Psalm 23:1

For You are my hope, Lord GOD,
my confidence from my youth. I have
leaned on You from birth. . . . My praise
is always about You.

Psalm 71:5-6

I will praise You forever for what You
have done.

Psalm 52:9

Worshiping God can be as loud and long as you want it to be.
Singing, clapping, whatever you're doing, don't let anything keep you from praising the Lord.

I will sing of Your strength and will joyfully proclaim Your faithful love.

Psalm 59:16

How good it is to sing to our God, for praise is pleasant and lovely.

Psalm 147:1

I will praise you every day.

Psalm 145:2

Worship is more than just feeling good, though. It's serious business. *This is the Maker of the universe we're talking about, not some big buddy of ours in the sky. He deserves our full respect.*

Look up and see: who created these?
He brings out the starry host by number;
He calls all of them by name.

Isaiah 40:26

Whom do I have in heaven but You?
And I desire nothing on earth but You.

Psalm 73:25

Come, let us worship and bow down;
let us kneel before the LORD our Maker.

Psalm 95:6

Serve the LORD with gladness;
  come before Him with joyful songs.
Acknowledge that the LORD is God.
  He made us, and we are His—
  His people, the sheep of His pasture.
Enter His gates with thanksgiving
  and His courts with praise.
Give thanks to Him
  and praise His name.
For the LORD is good,
  and His love is eternal;
His faithfulness endures
  through all generations.

Psalm 100:2-5

There is no such thing as a day that worshiping God won't make better. *Every morning when you get up, every time you pull a sandwich from your lunch bag, every day of your life—praise Him!*

I will sing about the LORD's faithful love forever.

Psalm 89:1

I will praise the LORD at all times; His praise will always be on my lips.

Psalm 34:1

This God, our God forever and ever— He will lead us eternally.

Psalm 48:14

Bowing in Prayer

You're Listening, Aren't You, God?

God has listened;
  He has paid attention
    to the sound of my prayer.
      May God be praised!
        He has not turned away.

Psalm 66:19-20

Your Father is as near as your next thought, already here to help you. *Praying to Him is something you can do anywhere you are—anytime you want—about anything you're up against.*

Whatever you ask in My name, I will do it, so that the Father may be glorified in the Son.

John 14:13

Even before they call, I will answer; while they are still speaking, I will hear.

Isaiah 65:24

Now this is the confidence we have before Him.

1 John 5:14

You don't have to be in trouble to pray. But if you are, then go ahead. *Call out to Him with your problems. He'll help you get through them the best way possible.*

Is anyone among you suffering? He should pray.

James 5:13

My God will hear me.

Micah 7:7

Help us, O LORD our God, for we depend on You.

2 Chronicles 14:11

The biggest reason to pray is not to beg, but just to be with God.
You are always welcome in His presence, always within reach of His love and care, always in His plans and on His mind.

Keep asking, and it will be given to you. Keep searching, and you will find. Keep knocking, and the door will be opened to you. For everyone who asks receives, and the one who searches finds, and to the one who knocks, the door will be opened.

Matthew 7:7-8

Therefore let us approach the throne of grace with boldness, so that we may receive mercy and find grace to help us at the proper time.

Hebrews 4:16

You should pray like this:
  "Our Father in heaven,
    Your name be honored as holy.
  Your kingdom come.
    Your will be done
    on earth as it is in heaven.
  Give us today our daily bread.
  And forgive us our debts,
    as we also have forgiven our debtors.
  And do not bring us into temptation,
    but deliver us from the evil one.
  For Yours is the kingdom and
    the power and the glory forever.
      Amen."

Matthew 6:9-13

Start praying while you're young. It's a friendship you'll never outgrow. *Whether you're praying for help, praying for others, or praying just to tell God how great He is, praying is always worth it.*

Pray for those who mistreat you.

Luke 6:28

Pray that you may not enter into temptation.

Luke 22:40

Brothers, pray for us.

1 Thessalonians 5:25

Pray constantly.

1 Thessalonians 5:17

Reading the Bible

If God Is Talking, I Need to Hear Him

Help me understand
  Your instruction,
    and I will obey it and
      follow it with all my heart.

Psalm 119:34

It may seem like an ordinary book. **But oh, it's much more than that!** *Take it from people like King David, who wrote the verses on this page. The Bible is worth more than all books put together!*

Instruction from Your lips is better for me than thousands of gold and silver pieces.

Psalm 119:72

They are more desirable than gold— than an abundance of pure gold; and sweeter than honey—than honey dripping from the comb. In addition, Your servant is warned by them; there is great reward in keeping them.

Psalm 19:10-11

What makes the Bible great is that
it never grows old. It's always new.
*People have been reading it for years, and
yet it always seems to say just what we
need to hear.*

The testimony of the LORD is trust-
worthy, making the inexperienced wise.

Psalm 19:7

The word of God is living and effective.

Hebrews 4:12

Practice these things . . . so that your
progress may be evident to all.

1 Timothy 4:15

The Bible is truly God's word to us. It is His voice speaking His truth. *It tells you who God is, what He's like, what He does. It tells you about what you can become in life. It tells you everything!*

Man does not live on bread alone but on every word that comes from the mouth of the LORD.

Deuteronomy 8:3

As for you, continue in what you have learned and firmly believed, knowing those from whom you learned, and that from childhood you have known the sacred Scriptures, which are able to instruct you for salvation through faith in Christ Jesus.

2 Timothy 3:14-16

Everyone who hears these words of Mine and acts on them will be like a sensible man who built his house on the rock. The rain fell, the rivers rose, and the winds blew and pounded that house. Yet it didn't collapse, because its foundation was on the rock.

But everyone who hears these words of Mine and doesn't act on them will be like a foolish man who built his house on the sand. The rain fell, the rivers rose, the winds blew and pounded that house . . . and its collapse was great!

Matthew 7:24-27

The best way to gain a love for the Bible is to start enjoying it yourself. *Notice how many times you've seen verses from Psalm 119 the last few pages. Turn there in your own Bible, and read on.*

Open my eyes so that I may see wonderful things in Your law.

Psalm 119:18

I delight to do Your will, my God; Your instruction resides within me.

Psalm 40:8

I am resolved to obey Your statutes to the very end.

Psalm 119:112

Believing in God

Lord, I Want to Be a Christian

These are written so that you
may believe Jesus is the Messiah,
the Son of God, and by believing
you may have life in His name.

John 20:31

God has made plans for you to have the most incredible life there is. *Living as a believer in Jesus Christ is like getting a lifetime guarantee—a promise that God will be working for your good.*

God loved the world in this way: He gave His One and Only Son, so that everyone who believes in Him will not perish but have eternal life.

John 3:16

I have come that they may have life and have it in abundance.

John 10:10

In Your presence is abundant joy; in Your right hand are eternal pleasures.

Psalm 16:11

But there's one big problem first: We don't deserve anything from God. *We were born in big trouble, and unless God does something incredible, we'll never get out of it.*

There is no one who does good.

Psalm 14:3

All have sinned and fall short of the glory of God.

Romans 3:23

Your sins have made Him hide His face from you.

Isaiah 59:2

Guess what, though? What we couldn't do, Jesus Christ did for us. *He came to earth with this one mission in mind: to die for our sins, to pay the huge debt we owed, to give us reason to hope.*

But God proves His own love for us in that while we were still sinners Christ died for us!

Romans 5:8

This is how we have come to know love: He laid down His life for us.

1 John 3:16

No one has greater love than this, that someone would lay down his life for his friends.

John 15:13

This is the message of faith that we proclaim: if you confess with your mouth, "Jesus is Lord," and believe in your heart that God raised Him from the dead, you will be saved.

With the heart one believes, resulting in righteousness, and with the mouth one confesses, resulting in salvation.

Now the Scripture says, "No one who believes on Him will be put to shame.... For everyone who calls on the name of the Lord will be saved."

Romans 10:8-11, 13

Will you believe in Him and give
your life to Him? Don't be afraid.
*Talk to your parents, your pastor, or your
teacher, and let them tell you more about
what it means to be a follower of Christ.*

Indeed, God is my salvation. I will trust
Him and not be afraid.

Isaiah 12:2

Don't be afraid, little flock, because
your Father delights to give you the
kingdom.

Luke 12:32

Don't be afraid. Only believe.

Mark 5:36

*Look for these other Bible Promise books
to give to the special people in your life.*

**Bible Promises
for Mom**
0-8054-2732-5

**Bible Promises
for Dad**
0-8054-2733-3

**Bible Promises
for My Teacher**
0-8054-2734-1

**Bible Promises
for the Graduate**
0-8054-2741-4

**Bible Promises
for New Believers**
0-8054-2742-2

**Bible Promises
for New Parents**
0-8054-2738-4

**Bible Promises
for Kids**
0-8054-2740-6

**Bible Promises
for Teens**
0-8054-2739-2